SNAPCHAT ADS BLUEPRINT

Your Strategy For Unmatched Marketing Impact

Hillary Jones

Icon Publications Limited

CONTENTS

INTRODUCTION

In a world where digital landscapes evolve at the speed of a swipe, mastering the art of advertising is not just a skill—it's a necessity. Welcome to "Snapchat Ads Blueprint: Your Strategy For Unmatched Marketing Impact," where we embark on an expedition through the dynamic realm of Snapchat advertising.

In the past decade, Snapchat has transformed from a simple messaging app to a cultural phenomenon, captivating the attention of millions worldwide. Its visual storytelling prowess and unparalleled engagement have made it a treasure trove for marketers seeking to reach audiences in innovative ways. This book is your compass to navigate this ever-evolving landscape, helping you unlock the full potential of Snapchat's advertising platform.

As we journey together through these pages, you'll gain not only the technical know-how but also the strategic insight required to orchestrate impactful Snapchat ad campaigns. Whether you're a seasoned marketer looking to expand your arsenal or a business owner eager to connect with a younger, digitally-savvy audience, this guide is designed to cater to your needs.

CHAPTER 1: EMBARKING ON YOUR SNAPCHAT ADVERTISING JOURNEY

Introduction To Snapchat's Dynamic Advertising Platform

Snapchat's dynamic advertising platform offers businesses a dynamic and engaging way to connect with their target audience. By utilizing this platform, companies can create and deliver personalized advertisements that adapt to users' preferences and behaviors in real-time. This innovative approach enables brands to showcase their products or services in a more relevant and appealing manner, fostering deeper user engagement and potentially driving higher conversion rates. Snapchat's dynamic advertising platform empowers advertisers to tailor their content based on factors such as location, interests, and demographics, enhancing the overall effectiveness of their marketing campaigns on the platform.

Overview Of The Potential Benefits And Reach

Snapchat ads offer a range of potential benefits and a wide-reaching platform for businesses aiming to connect with their target audience. With a user base comprising millions of active users, Snapchat provides a vast and diverse audience to showcase products and services. The platform's immersive ad formats, including filters, lenses, and vertical videos, enable brands to create captivating and memorable experiences that resonate with users.

One of the notable advantages of Snapchat ads is their potential for high engagement. The platform's interactive features encourage users to swipe, tap, and explore content, fostering a deeper connection between brands and consumers. This engagement can lead to increased brand awareness and even viral sharing, amplifying the reach of campaigns.

Snapchat's ad targeting capabilities are another significant benefit. Advertisers can finely tune their campaigns based on factors like demographics, location, interests, and behaviors, ensuring their content is delivered to the right people at the right time. This precision targeting enhances the likelihood of resonating with users who are more likely to convert.

Furthermore, Snapchat offers valuable insights through its analytics tools. Advertisers can track metrics such as views, engagement rates, and conversion data, allowing them to assess the performance of their campaigns and make informed optimizations.

Incorporating Snapchat ads into a marketing strategy can lead to increased brand exposure, engagement, and potential conversions, all while leveraging the platform's unique and dynamic features to stand out in a crowded digital landscape.

The Evolution Of Snapchat As A Marketing Channel

Over the years, Snapchat has undergone a noteworthy evolution as a dynamic marketing channel, adapting to changing trends and user behaviors. Initially introduced as a platform primarily for ephemeral messaging, Snapchat gradually recognized its potential as a marketing tool and evolved to accommodate brands' promotional efforts.

The introduction of sponsored geofilters and lenses marked Snapchat's initial foray into advertising. Brands began to leverage these interactive elements to engage users creatively, increasing brand visibility and fostering a sense of playfulness in marketing campaigns.

As the platform evolved further, it introduced full-screen vertical video ads that seamlessly integrated with user-generated content. This format allowed brands to deliver more immersive and captivating experiences, grabbing users' attention in a mobile-first world.

Snapchat's "Discover" section played a pivotal role in its marketing evolution by allowing publishers and brands to share editorial content, thereby establishing a content-rich environment for users beyond personal communication. This feature facilitated the integration of branded content in a way that felt less intrusive and more aligned with user interests.

The subsequent launch of the "Snapchat Ads Manager" provided advertisers with more sophisticated targeting options and measurement tools. This evolution empowered brands to tailor their campaigns to specific demographics, locations, and even retarget users who had previously engaged with their content.

Snapchat's evolution continued with the introduction of augmented reality (AR) advertising. Brands could create interactive AR experiences, allowing users to virtually interact with products before making purchasing decisions. This innovative approach to advertising brought a new level of engagement and excitement to marketing efforts.

In essence, Snapchat's journey as a marketing channel has evolved from simple geofilters and lenses to a comprehensive platform offering a diverse array of advertising options. Its focus on user engagement, interactive content, and personalized experiences has positioned it as a valuable channel for brands aiming to connect with younger audiences in a creative and meaningful way.

* * *

CHAPTER 2: NAVIGATING THE SNAPCHAT ECOSYSTEM

Creating Your Business Account: Step-By-Step Walkthrough

Here's a step-by-step walkthrough for creating a business account for Snapchat ads:

Step 1: Sign Up
Visit the Snapchat for Business website (business.snapchat.com).
Click on "Get Started" or "Sign Up" to begin the process.

Step 2: Account Information
Enter your email address and create a password for your business account.
Provide your business name and select your country/region.

Step 3: Business Details
Enter your business website URL.
Choose the industry that best represents your business from the provided list.

Step 4: Contact Information
Fill in your business contact information, including a phone number.

Step 5: Verification
Verify your email address by clicking on the verification link sent to the email you provided.

Step 6: Ad Account Setup
Choose whether you're setting up an ad account for your business or an agency.
Provide your business name and billing information.

Step 7: Ad Account Settings
Define your ad account's time zone and currency.
Set up your ad preferences, including targeting options and ad types.

Step 8: Payment Setup
Enter your payment details, including credit card information, to pay for your ads.

Step 9: Confirmation
Review all the information you've provided.
If everything looks correct, click on "Create Account" or a similar button to finalize the setup.

Step 10: Explore Ad Manager
Once your business account is set up, you'll be directed to the Ad Manager dashboard.

Here, you can start creating campaigns, designing ads, and managing your advertising efforts on Snapchat.
Remember, the steps and interface might change slightly over time as Snapchat updates its platform, so it's a good idea to refer to Snapchat's official resources or guides for the most accurate and up-to-date instructions.

Familiarizing Yourself With The Snapchat Ads Manager Interface

To become acquainted with the Snapchat Ads Manager interface and its functionalities in an original manner, consider the following approach:

Exploring the Snapchat Ads Manager Interface: A Personalized Guide

Getting started with the Snapchat Ads Manager interface can be an exciting journey. To navigate this platform effectively and gain a comprehensive understanding of its features, follow these tailored steps:

Create Your Snapchat Account:
If you haven't already, sign up for a Snapchat account. This will grant you access to the Ads Manager interface, a hub for managing your ad campaigns.

Access the Ads Manager:
Once logged in, locate the Snapchat Ads Manager. This can usually be found by clicking on your profile icon or by searching "Ads Manager" in Snapchat's search bar.

Unveil the Interface:
Delve into the different sections of the Ads Manager interface. Spend time familiarizing yourself with the layout, tabs, and menus. Key areas to focus on include:

Dashboard/Home: This serves as an overview of your campaigns, expenditures, and performance metrics.

Campaigns: Here's where you create and manage your ad campaigns.

Ad Sets: Tailor your targeting, budget, and schedule for each campaign.

Ads: Create and manage the actual ads within your ad sets.

Reports: Gain insights into campaign performance.

Tools: Discover additional features for optimizing your ads.
Engage with Guided Tours (if Available):
Snapchat may offer guided tours or tutorials when you access the Ads Manager. These can provide a hands-on introduction to key features and

functions.

Consult Official Documentation and Guides:
Snapchat provides official documentation, guides, and tutorials. Dive into these resources to gain in-depth insights into every aspect of the Ads Manager. Topics such as campaign creation, ad formats, targeting strategies, budget allocation, and optimization techniques are worth exploring.

Leverage Video Tutorials:
Video tutorials, often available on platforms like YouTube, offer visual guides by marketing experts. These tutorials walk you through the process of utilizing the Ads Manager effectively.

Immerse Yourself in Practical Exercises:
Experiment with sample campaigns using a modest budget. This hands-on approach helps you gain confidence in navigating the interface without committing substantial resources.

Participate in Digital Communities:
Join online forums, Facebook groups, or relevant subreddits where marketers exchange insights on Snapchat advertising. Engage in discussions, ask questions, and learn from others' experiences.

Stay Abreast of Updates:
The digital advertising landscape is dynamic. Keep yourself informed about new features, changes, and best practices. Follow official Snapchat announcements, industry blogs, and news sources.

Embrace Iteration and Analysis:
As you grow more adept with the interface, experiment with diverse campaign types, ad formats, targeting options, and optimization strategies. Continuously evaluate campaign performance to refine your approach.

Embarking on this journey to mastery may take time, but with perseverance and consistent learning, you'll gain the expertise needed to navigate the Snapchat Ads Manager interface effectively.

Linking And Managing Business Assets Effectively

When it comes to linking and efficiently managing business assets for Snapchat ads, the process involves a systematic approach to ensure a seamless and strategic campaign setup. Here's a personalized guide on how to achieve this while maintaining originality:

Strategically Linking and Managing Business Assets for Successful Snapchat Ads

Integrating and managing business assets for Snapchat ads requires a structured method to achieve a coherent and effective advertising strategy. To establish this linkage and manage assets proficiently, follow these tailored steps:

Understand Your Business Objectives:
Begin by clarifying your business goals. Whether it's driving website traffic, increasing app installs, or boosting brand awareness, align your asset management strategy with your objectives.

Access Snapchat Business Manager:
Log into Snapchat Business Manager, the central hub for managing your advertising assets. From your profile, access the Business Manager interface to initiate the process.

Add and Verify Your Business:
If your business isn't already added, do so by providing accurate information. Follow the verification process to ensure your business is recognized and trusted by Snapchat.

Connect Ad Accounts:
Link your relevant ad accounts to the Business Manager. This step streamlines the management of multiple accounts and enables effective allocation of budgets and assets.

Integrate Pixels and Events:
Implement Snapchat Pixel on your website. This allows you to track user interactions, optimize campaigns, and measure conversions. Configure pixel events to capture specific actions users take on your site.

Manage Product Catalogs:
If you're running e-commerce campaigns, organize and upload your product catalog. Regularly update it to reflect the latest offerings, prices, and availability.

Create Asset Libraries:
Use Snapchat's asset libraries to centralize your creative elements, like images, videos, and ad copies. This simplifies the process of creating and launching ads by providing easy access to visuals.

Set Up Business Locations:
For brick-and-mortar businesses, add and manage your business locations. This facilitates localized targeting and provides users with relevant information.

Collaborate with Team Members:
If you're working with a team, assign roles and permissions within Business Manager. This ensures that the right individuals have access to specific assets and campaigns.

Explore Dynamic Ads:
Utilize Snapchat's dynamic ads feature to automatically generate personalized ads based on user behavior and preferences. This enhances engagement and conversion rates.

Regularly Review and Optimize:
Continuously analyze campaign performance using the data provided by Snapchat Pixel. Adjust your strategies based on insights gained to improve ad effectiveness.

Stay Updated on Platform Changes:

Snapchat's features and functionalities evolve. Stay informed about updates, new ad formats, and best practices to remain competitive and make the most of available tools.

Test and Iterate:
Experiment with different ad formats, targeting options, and creative elements. A/B testing helps you identify what resonates best with your target audience.

Seek Professional Guidance:
If needed, consider consulting with Snapchat experts or agencies to optimize your asset management strategy and achieve better results.

By approaching the process of linking and managing business assets for Snapchat ads systematically, you'll be well-equipped to create compelling campaigns, reach your target audience effectively, and achieve your advertising goals.

* * *

CHAPTER 3: STRATEGY BLUEPRINT: MAPPING YOUR SNAPCHAT ADVERTISING APPROACH

Defining Clear Marketing Goals And Objectives

Deconstructing Your Target Audience: Demographics And Behaviors

Deconstructing your target audience, demographics, and behaviors for Snapchat ads involves a strategic approach to ensure effective targeting and engagement. Here's how you can go about it:

1. Define Your Audience:
Start by clearly defining your target audience. Consider factors such as age, gender, location, and interests. Determine whether your product or service is more appealing to a specific demographic group.

2. Leverage Snapchat Insights:
Utilize Snapchat Insights to gather data about your existing followers, including demographics and engagement metrics. This information can

offer valuable insights into the characteristics of your current audience.

3. Conduct Market Research:
Conduct thorough market research to understand your industry, competition, and trends. This research can help you identify gaps in the market and tailor your messaging to resonate with your target audience's needs.

4. Analyze Competitors:
Study your competitors' Snapchat presence. Look at the type of content they post, the engagement they receive, and the audience they seem to attract. This analysis can provide insights into effective strategies and audience preferences.

5. Utilize Audience Insights:
Leverage Snapchat's ad platform to access audience insights. Explore data on interests, behaviors, and lifestyles of Snapchat users. This information can help you refine your targeting parameters.

6. Create User Personas:
Develop detailed user personas representing different segments of your target audience. Include information such as age, occupation, hobbies, pain points, and goals. This will help you visualize and understand your audience better.

7. Use A/B Testing:
When running ad campaigns, use A/B testing to experiment with different ad creatives, messages, and targeting parameters. This can help you identify which elements resonate most with your audience and refine your approach.

8. Monitor Analytics:
Regularly monitor the analytics of your Snapchat ads. Track metrics like click-through rates, engagement rates, and conversions. Analyzing this data will allow you to adjust your strategy based on real-time insights.

9. Iterate and Refine:

Based on the data and insights you gather, continuously iterate and refine your targeting strategy. Adjust your audience parameters, ad content, and messaging to align with what performs best.

10. Seek Feedback:
Engage with your Snapchat audience by seeking feedback through surveys, polls, or interactive features. This direct interaction can provide you with qualitative insights into your audience's preferences and opinions.

By following these steps, you'll be able to systematically deconstruct your target audience, demographics, and behaviors on Snapchat. This will enable you to create more relevant, personalized, and effective ad campaigns that resonate with the right users.

Crafting A Holistic Strategy That Aligns With Your Brand Identity

Crafting a holistic Snapchat ads strategy that aligns with your brand identity requires careful planning and consideration. Here's a step-by-step approach to help you create a strategy that effectively reflects your brand:

1. Define Your Brand Identity:
Clarify your brand's values, mission, and unique selling points. Understand what sets your brand apart and how you want to be perceived by your target audience.

2. Understand Your Audience:
Thoroughly research and analyze your target audience's preferences, behaviors, and interests. Tailor your strategy to resonate with their needs and aspirations.

3. Set Clear Objectives:
Determine what you aim to achieve with your Snapchat ads. Whether it's brand awareness, lead generation, or sales, having clear objectives will guide your strategy.

4. Choose Ad Formats:

Select Snapchat ad formats that align with your brand's style and messaging. Whether it's Story Ads, Lenses, Filters, or Collection Ads, choose formats that best showcase your products/services.

5. Craft Compelling Content:

Develop creative content that reflects your brand's tone, values, and visual identity. Ensure your ad visuals, copy, and messaging are consistent with your overall brand messaging.

6. Design for Mobile:

Keep in mind that Snapchat is a mobile-first platform. Design ads that are visually appealing and easy to consume on mobile devices. Use vertical formats for optimal viewing.

7. Personalize and Contextualize:

Utilize Snapchat's targeting options to personalize ads based on user demographics, behaviors, and preferences. Craft messages that feel relevant and resonate with individual users.

8. Create a Content Calendar:

Plan a content calendar that outlines when and what type of content you'll be posting. This ensures a consistent presence and prevents ad fatigue.

9. Focus on Storytelling:

Use storytelling techniques to convey your brand's narrative through your ads. Engage users emotionally and connect your products/services to their lives.

10. Test and Optimize:

Run A/B tests to experiment with different ad elements, such as visuals, copy, and calls to action. Continuously analyze results and optimize your strategy based on performance data.

11. Maintain Consistency:

Ensure that your Snapchat ads align with your brand's messaging on other platforms. Consistency across all touchpoints reinforces your brand identity.

12. Monitor and Measure:
Regularly monitor ad performance metrics such as engagement rates, conversion rates, and return on ad spend (ROAS). Adjust your strategy based on what works best.

13. Embrace Creativity:
Snapchat is a creative platform. Don't be afraid to experiment with innovative ideas, AR experiences, and interactive content that resonate with your brand.

14. Evolve and Adapt:
Stay open to adapting your strategy based on changing trends, audience feedback, and platform updates. A dynamic approach ensures your strategy remains relevant.

By following these steps, you can create a holistic Snapchat ads strategy that not only aligns with your brand identity but also effectively engages your target audience and drives meaningful results.

* * *

CHAPTER 4: CRAFTING CAPTIVATING AD CREATIVES

Unlocking The Vertical Canvas: Art Of Visual Storytelling

Unlocking the vertical canvas in the art of visual storytelling for Snapchat ads involves leveraging the platform's unique features to create engaging and immersive narratives. Here's how you can do it:

1. Embrace Vertical Format:
Snapchat's vertical orientation is tailor-made for mobile devices. Use this format to your advantage by designing visuals and videos that fit seamlessly within the vertical canvas, optimizing user experience.

2. Capture Attention Quickly:
Start your story with a captivating visual or intriguing message within the first few seconds. The vertical format demands quick attention-grabbing content to prevent users from swiping away.

3. Use Motion Creatively:
Take advantage of the vertical canvas to incorporate motion, animations, and transitions that guide users through your narrative. Movement can enhance engagement and draw viewers deeper into your story.

4. Visual Continuity:

Maintain visual consistency throughout your story. Use colors, fonts, and design elements that align with your brand identity, creating a cohesive and recognizable experience.

5. Break the Story into Segments:

Divide your narrative into segments or scenes, each building on the previous one. This helps create anticipation and a sense of progression as users swipe through your content.

6. Leverage Vertical Split Screens:

Snapchat allows you to create split-screen visuals within a vertical canvas. Use this feature to show contrasting or complementary visuals side by side, enhancing your storytelling.

7. Incorporate Text and Graphics:

Overlay text and graphics strategically to provide context, emphasize key points, or add a touch of creativity. Just ensure that they don't clutter the visual space.

8. Create Interactive Experiences:

Utilize Snapchat's interactive features, such as lenses, filters, and interactive swipe-ups. These elements encourage users to engage directly with your content, enhancing the storytelling experience.

9. Use Sound and Music:

Sound plays a vital role in storytelling. Incorporate sound effects, music, or even narration to enhance the emotional impact of your visuals.

10. Evoke Emotion:

Craft a narrative that evokes emotion. Whether it's humor, inspiration, empathy, or excitement, emotions can help users connect with your brand on a deeper level.

11. Maintain Conciseness:

Given the limited attention span on mobile platforms, keep your storytelling concise and focused. Deliver your message efficiently within a short timeframe.

12. Experiment with AR:
Leverage Snapchat's augmented reality capabilities to create interactive and immersive experiences. AR elements can enhance user engagement and make your storytelling more memorable.

13. Test and Iterate:
Run A/B tests to evaluate different storytelling approaches. Analyze engagement metrics to determine what resonates best with your audience and refine your strategy accordingly.

14. Optimize for Vertical Scrolling:
Keep in mind that users will scroll vertically through your story. Design your narrative to ensure that each part of the story flows smoothly as users progress.

By embracing the vertical canvas, utilizing interactive features, and crafting a compelling narrative, you can create Snapchat ads that captivate your audience and effectively convey your brand's message.

Design Principles For Attention-Grabbing Snaps And Videos

When creating attention-grabbing snaps and videos for Snapchat ads, it's essential to apply effective design principles that capture users' interest and hold their attention. Here are some design principles to utilize:

1. Visual Clarity:
Ensure that your visuals are clear and easy to understand at a glance. Avoid clutter and use high-quality images or videos that communicate your message clearly.

2. Bold Colors and Contrast:

Utilize bold and vibrant colors that stand out in users' feeds. Contrast between elements can help highlight key information and create visual impact.

3. Compelling Thumbnail:
Snapchat ads often start with a thumbnail. Make sure this initial frame is visually captivating and intriguing, encouraging users to click and view the full content.

4. Clear Focal Point:
Place the most important element or message in a prominent position within your snap or video. This helps guide users' attention and reinforces the main point of your ad.

5. Minimal Text:
Keep text concise and to the point. Avoid overwhelming users with excessive text. Use text to complement visuals, not replace them.

6. Quick Visual Cues:
Incorporate visual cues that immediately convey the purpose or benefit of your ad. Users should understand the value proposition in seconds.

7. Movement and Animation:
Utilize movement, animations, or GIFs to create dynamic visuals that catch the eye and encourage users to engage with your content.

8. Storytelling Sequence:
If your ad tells a story, structure it in a sequence of snaps or frames that unfold in a logical and engaging manner. Each frame should build anticipation for the next.

9. User-Centric Approach:
Design your content with your target audience in mind. Use imagery, language, and visuals that resonate with their preferences and interests.

10. Creative Use of Filters and Lenses:

Leverage Snapchat's filters and lenses creatively to enhance your visuals and make your content more interactive and entertaining.

11. Utilize Negative Space:

Negative space can help emphasize your main subject and create a visually pleasing composition. Don't be afraid to leave areas of your snap or video uncluttered.

12. Dynamic Typography:

If using text, experiment with different font styles and sizes to create hierarchy and visual interest. Typography can contribute to the overall design aesthetic.

13. Seamless Looping:

If your ad is a video, consider creating a seamless loop that encourages users to watch the content multiple times.

14. Consistent Branding:

Maintain consistent branding elements such as logo placement, color scheme, and font choices to reinforce your brand identity.

15. Test and Iterate:

Run A/B tests with different design elements to determine which visuals and approaches generate the highest engagement. Continuously refine your designs based on user feedback.

By applying these design principles, you can create captivating Snapchat ads that effectively grab users' attention, convey your message, and drive engagement with your brand.

Incorporating Branding Elements That Resonate

Incorporating branding elements that resonate within your Snapchat ads involves a thoughtful approach that aligns your brand identity with the platform's unique features. Here's how you can effectively integrate branding elements:

1. Consistent Visual Identity:
Ensure your Snapchat ads reflect your brand's visual identity, including colors, fonts, and logo placement. Consistency helps users recognize your brand instantly.

2. Seamless Integration:
Integrate branding elements seamlessly into the ad's design. The goal is to make them feel like a natural part of the content rather than intrusive additions.

3. Logo Placement:
Place your logo strategically within the ad, preferably in a corner or area that doesn't obstruct the main content. Make sure it's visible without overpowering the message.

4. Brand Colors:
Incorporate your brand colors in a way that complements the overall design. Colors should resonate with your brand's personality and evoke the desired emotions.

5. Typography:
Use typography that aligns with your brand's tone. Whether it's bold and modern or elegant and classic, the font should reinforce your brand's character.

6. Brand Voice:
Craft ad copy using your brand's unique voice and language. The tone should be consistent with how your brand communicates across other channels.

7. Storytelling Alignment:
Incorporate branding elements into the narrative of your ad. Make them an integral part of the story to create a more immersive and resonant experience.

8. Product Placement:
If showcasing a product, position it in a way that highlights its features
while still adhering to your brand's visual guidelines.

9. Call-to-Action (CTA):
Design your CTA button with your brand's aesthetics in mind. Use a
consistent style for buttons, encouraging users to take the desired action.

10. Personalization:
Tailor your ad to resonate with different audience segments. Customize
branding elements based on user demographics and interests to enhance
relevancy.

11. Highlight Brand Values:
If applicable, incorporate elements that showcase your brand's values,
mission, or social responsibility efforts. This can create a stronger
emotional connection.

12. Avoid Overloading:
While it's important to showcase branding, avoid overwhelming the ad with
too many elements. Maintain a balanced design that doesn't distract from
the main message.

13. Feedback and Testing:
Seek feedback from your target audience or internal team to ensure that the
branding elements resonate effectively. Run tests to assess how users
respond to the incorporation of branding.

14. Continual Refinement:
As you gather data and insights from ad performance, refine your branding
strategy. Adapt based on what resonates best with your audience and drives
desired outcomes.

*By thoughtfully incorporating branding elements that resonate, you
can create Snapchat ads that not only capture attention but also*

leave a lasting impression of your brand in the minds of users.

* * *

CHAPTER 5: CHOOSING THE RIGHT AD FORMAT FOR MAXIMUM IMPACT

Dive Into Snap Ads, Story Ads, Collection Ads, And More

Diving into different types of Snapchat ads, such as Snap Ads, Story Ads, and Collection Ads, requires understanding their unique features and tailoring your approach to match your marketing objectives. Here's a breakdown of these ad formats:

1. Snap Ads:
Snap Ads are full-screen vertical video ads that appear between users' stories or within the Discover section. These ads offer a few seconds of video content, along with an optional swipe-up CTA for more information.

2. Story Ads:
Story Ads allow you to create a sequence of 3-20 snaps that users can swipe through. This format is ideal for telling a sequential narrative or showcasing different aspects of a product or service.

3. Collection Ads:
Collection Ads enable you to display a collection of products within a single ad unit. Users can tap on individual products to view more details or make a purchase.

4. Filters and Lenses:

Filters and Lenses are interactive elements that users can apply to their own content. Sponsored filters and lenses allow you to create branded interactive experiences that users can engage with.

5. Dynamic Ads:

Dynamic Ads automatically create multiple ads featuring different products from your product catalog. These ads are tailored to users based on their interests and behaviors.

6. Commercials:

Commercials are non-skippable, full-screen vertical video ads that play in the Discover feed. They are best for capturing users' undivided attention.

7. Augmented Reality (AR) Ads:

AR Ads allow users to interact with your brand's products in augmented reality. Users can experience and visualize products in their real-world environment.

8. App Install Ads:

App Install Ads are designed to drive app installations. Users can swipe up to install your app directly from the ad.

9. Web View Ads:

Web View Ads allow users to access a mobile webpage from within the Snapchat app. They're useful for driving traffic to specific landing pages.

To get started with these ad formats:

Define Objectives: Determine your advertising goals, whether it's brand awareness, engagement, conversions, or app installs.

Select the Right Format: Choose the ad format that aligns with your objectives and the type of content you want to showcase.

Create Engaging Content: Craft visually appealing and engaging content that resonates with your target audience. Remember to consider the vertical orientation and mobile-first design.

Utilize Targeting: Leverage Snapchat's targeting options to reach your desired audience based on demographics, interests, behaviors, and more.

Set a Budget: Determine your budget and bidding strategy for your ads.

Monitor and Optimize: Regularly track ad performance metrics and make adjustments based on the data you gather. Test different creatives and targeting options to find what works best.

Experiment and Iterate: Don't hesitate to experiment with different ad formats and strategies. Continuously refine your approach based on results.

By exploring these various ad formats and tailoring your strategy to your goals, you can effectively leverage Snapchat ads to reach and engage your target audience.

Tailoring Ad Formats To Diverse Campaign Objectives

Tailoring Snapchat ad formats to diverse campaign objectives involves understanding the strengths of each format and selecting the one that aligns best with your specific goals. Here's how to adapt ad formats to different campaign objectives:

1. Brand Awareness:

Choose formats that capture attention quickly, such as Snap Ads or Commercials.
Focus on delivering a concise and memorable message that showcases your brand's personality.
Incorporate your brand elements early in the ad to increase brand recall.

2. Engagement and Interaction:

Utilize interactive formats like Filters, Lenses, and AR Ads to encourage users to engage with your content.
Create engaging and playful experiences that resonate with your target audience.
Prompt users to share their experiences with friends, boosting organic reach.

3. Conversions and Sales:

Opt for formats that allow direct action, like Collection Ads or Web View Ads.
Showcase specific products, highlight their features, and provide a clear call-to-action (CTA) for users to take the next step.
Utilize retargeting options to reach users who have previously interacted with your brand.

4. App Installs and Downloads:

Choose App Install Ads that drive users to download your app directly.
Highlight the key benefits and features of your app to encourage installations.
Offer special promotions or incentives to attract users to download.

5. Storytelling and Product Showcase:

Story Ads or Collection Ads are great for telling a sequential story or showcasing a range of products.
Use a series of snaps to build a narrative that engages users and maintains their interest.
Highlight different aspects of your products or services in each snap.

6. Local or Event Promotion:

Employ Geofilters or Sponsored Lenses to create location-specific experiences for users.
Incorporate branding elements and event-related imagery to tie into the local context.
Encourage users to share their experiences at the event or location.

7. Follower Growth and Engagement:
Create engaging content within your Story or Snap Ads that resonates with your target audience.
Showcase behind-the-scenes content, company culture, or user-generated content to foster a sense of community.
Include a CTA that encourages users to follow your account for more content.

8. Education and Awareness:
Use Snap Ads to deliver educational content in a concise and engaging manner.
Incorporate visuals, animations, or short videos to explain concepts effectively.
Drive users to learn more on your website or through a Web View Ad.

9. Social Responsibility Campaigns:
Leverage Snapchat's interactive features to create impactful and emotionally resonant AR experiences.
Tell powerful stories that convey your brand's commitment to social causes.
Encourage users to participate or take action to support the cause.
By aligning the strengths of different Snapchat ad formats with your campaign objectives, you can create more effective and impactful ads that resonate with your audience and drive the desired outcomes.

Strategic Insights For Optimizing Each Format's Potential

Optimizing each Snapchat ad format's potential requires a strategic approach that leverages the unique features of each format. Here's how you can maximize the effectiveness of various ad formats:

1. Snap Ads:
Quick Impact: Utilize the first few seconds to capture attention. Deliver a concise and compelling message that encourages users to swipe up for more information.

Clear CTA: Incorporate a clear call-to-action (CTA) that guides users on the next steps, whether it's to learn more, visit your website, or make a purchase.
Vertical Video: Leverage the vertical format to create visually engaging videos that fit seamlessly into users' feeds.

2. Story Ads:

Sequential Storytelling: Craft a cohesive narrative that unfolds across multiple snaps. Build anticipation with each snap, encouraging users to swipe through the story.
Variety and Consistency: Showcase different aspects of your brand, products, or services while maintaining a consistent visual theme throughout the story.
Strong Ending: Conclude with a powerful snap that reinforces your key message or includes a compelling CTA.

3. Collection Ads:

Product Showcase: Display a range of products within a single ad unit. Utilize visually appealing images to highlight each product's unique features.
Seamless Navigation: Ensure a seamless user experience by linking each product to a corresponding page for more information or purchase.
Compelling Thumbnails: Create captivating thumbnails that entice users to explore the collection further.

4. Filters and Lenses:

Interactive Engagement: Develop Filters and Lenses that encourage users to interact with your brand. Incorporate games, effects, or challenges that users can share.
Branded Experience: Infuse your brand's identity into the interactive elements, allowing users to engage while immersed in your brand's aesthetics.
Viral Sharing: Design experiences that users will want to share with friends, expanding your ad's reach organically.

5. Dynamic Ads:

Personalization: Utilize user data to show products or content relevant to each user's preferences and behaviors, increasing the likelihood of engagement.
Timely Messaging: Display ads based on users' recent interactions or interests to ensure relevancy and encourage immediate action.
Automated Creatives: Leverage automation to dynamically generate ad content, optimizing for each user's profile.

6. Commercials:

Compelling Story: Use the non-skippable format to tell a captivating story that resonates with users and delivers your message effectively.
Elevated Production: Invest in high-quality production to create visually stunning commercials that capture users' attention and deliver a memorable experience.
CTA Integration: Incorporate a strong CTA that encourages users to take action once the commercial ends.

7. AR Ads:

Interactive Experiences: Design AR Ads that allow users to interact with your products in their environment, creating a memorable and engaging experience.
Educational Content: Use AR to educate users about your products' features or benefits, making the learning process interactive and fun.
Social Sharing: Encourage users to share their AR experiences with friends, amplifying your ad's impact.

8. App Install and Web View Ads:

Clear Value Proposition: Highlight the key benefits of downloading your app or visiting your website in a concise and compelling manner.
CTA Urgency: Create a sense of urgency in your CTA to encourage users to take immediate action, such as installing the app or exploring the site.

By implementing these strategic insights for each Snapchat ad format, you can optimize their potential to effectively engage your audience, drive conversions, and achieve your campaign objectives.

* * *

CHAPTER 6: PRECISION TARGETING: REACHING THE RIGHT AUDIENCE

Mastering Demographic, Interest-Based, And Behavior-Driven Targeting

Mastering demographic, interest-based, and behavior-driven targeting for Snapchat ads requires a strategic approach that leverages the platform's targeting capabilities. Here's how you can effectively navigate these targeting options:

1. Demographic Targeting:

Define Your Audience: Clearly identify the demographics of your target audience, including age, gender, location, and language preferences.
Audience Insights: Utilize Snapchat's audience insights to understand the demographics of your current followers and users who engage with your content.
Customize Messaging: Tailor your ad content to resonate with the specific demographics you're targeting, addressing their needs and preferences.

2. Interest-Based Targeting:
Audience Research: Conduct thorough research to identify the interests, hobbies, and preferences of your target audience.

Interest Categories: Utilize Snapchat's interest categories to refine your targeting. Choose relevant categories that align with your products or services.

Personalized Content: Craft ad content that speaks directly to the interests of your audience, capturing their attention and sparking engagement.

3. Behavior-Driven Targeting:

Behavior Data: Leverage behavior data from Snapchat to understand users' past interactions, such as app installations, engagement with ads, and purchase behaviors.

Retargeting: Implement retargeting strategies to reach users who have engaged with your brand before. Show them relevant content or promotions based on their previous actions.

Lookalike Audiences: Create lookalike audiences based on the behavior patterns of your existing customers. This expands your reach to users with similar behaviors.

4. Custom Audiences:

Upload Lists: Utilize custom audiences by uploading customer email lists or mobile IDs. This enables you to target existing customers or engage with those who are already familiar with your brand.

Retain and Re-Engage: Target custom audiences with special offers, promotions, or exclusive content to encourage repeat business and re-engagement.

5. Geographic Targeting:

Local Focus: Utilize geofilters or location-based targeting to connect with users in specific locations, such as cities, regions, or even specific events.

Location Insights: Analyze location data to understand where your audience spends time. Tailor your messaging to resonate with their local context.

6. Creative Adaptation:

Personalize Content: Customize ad visuals and messaging based on the demographic, interests, and behaviors of your targeted audience.

Segmentation: Create different ad variations for various segments of your audience. This allows you to deliver more relevant content to each group.

7. Continuous Optimization:
Monitor Performance: Regularly review the performance of your ads and targeting parameters. Analyze metrics like engagement, click-through rates, and conversions.
Iterate and Refine: Based on performance data, make adjustments to your targeting strategy. Experiment with different combinations to find what resonates best.
By mastering demographic, interest-based, and behavior-driven targeting, you can create highly relevant and effective Snapchat ads that engage your target audience and drive desired outcomes for your campaigns.

Harnessing The Power Of Custom And Lookalike Audiences

Harnessing the power of custom and lookalike audiences in Snapchat ads involves using targeted audience segments to enhance your ad campaigns. Here's how you can effectively leverage these audience types:

Custom Audiences:

1. Customer Data Utilization:
Upload Customer Lists: Utilize customer data you've collected, such as email lists or mobile IDs, and upload them to Snapchat. This enables you to directly target your existing customer base.

2. Retain and Re-Engage:
Exclusive Offers: Design ad content that offers exclusive deals, promotions, or incentives to your existing customers. This encourages repeat business and reinforces brand loyalty.
Re-Engagement: Reach out to past customers who may not have interacted with your brand recently. Showcase new products or updates to reignite their interest.

3. Cross-Sell and Upsell:

Segmented Campaigns: Create segmented ad campaigns targeting different customer groups based on their purchase history or preferences.
Complementary Products: Showcase products that complement what customers have previously purchased, encouraging cross-selling opportunities.
Lookalike Audiences:

1. Expand Reach:
Identify High-Value Customers: Analyze your existing customer base to identify those who are most engaged or have high purchase frequency.
Create Lookalikes: Use these high-value customers as a basis to create lookalike audiences. Snapchat will find users with similar characteristics to target.

2. Target Similar Users:
Behavioral Patterns: Lookalike audiences target users who exhibit behaviors and preferences similar to your high-value customers.
Demographic Alignment: Ensure that the lookalike audience demographics align with your target market.

3. Campaign Optimization:
Performance Insights: Regularly analyze the performance of your lookalike audience campaigns. Monitor engagement, conversions, and other relevant metrics.
Adjust Targeting: If a specific lookalike audience isn't performing as expected, consider adjusting the criteria or focusing on other segments.

4. Creative Messaging:
Resonate with Similarities: Craft ad content that resonates with the interests and preferences of your high-value customers, as these will likely align with the lookalike audience.

5. Gradual Expansion:
Start Small: Begin by testing your lookalike audience campaigns on a smaller scale. Monitor performance before scaling up to a larger audience.

By harnessing custom and lookalike audiences effectively, you can reach the right users with tailored messages, expand your reach to new potential customers, and drive better results from your Snapchat ad campaigns.

Geo-Targeting Strategies For Localized And Global

Utilizing geo-targeting strategies effectively in Snapchat ads can help you reach specific audiences both locally and globally. Here's how you can employ these strategies:

Local Geo-Targeting:

Geofilters: Create location-specific geofilters that users can apply to their snaps. These filters can showcase your brand and promote local events, stores, or businesses.
Event Promotions: Use geofilters to target users attending local events, festivals, or conferences. This strategy enables you to engage with a relevant and captive audience.
Location-Based Offers: Design ads with special promotions available only to users within a certain radius of your physical store. Encourage foot traffic and in-store visits.
Local Insights: Utilize location data to understand where your target audience spends time. Tailor your ad content to align with their local interests and preferences.
Localized Messaging: Craft ad copy that incorporates local references, landmarks, or slang that resonates with the targeted region.
Global Geo-Targeting:

Country and Region Targeting:
Target specific countries, regions, or cities to reach a global audience while still narrowing down your scope.

Multilingual Campaigns: If targeting different language-speaking regions, create ads in the respective languages to enhance connection and comprehension.

Time Zone Consideration: Schedule ads to align with different time zones to ensure users receive content at optimal times in their region.

Cultural Relevance: Research cultural norms, holidays, and events in different regions. Tailor your ad content to align with cultural sensitivities and preferences.

Combining Local and Global:

Localized Global Campaigns: Craft ads that resonate with a global audience while incorporating elements that connect with local culture or references.

Localized Insights: Analyze how users in different regions engage with your content. Use these insights to optimize your ads for both local and global segments.

Event and Product Launches: Leverage both local and global geo-targeting for event or product launches. Create localized buzz while reaching a wider audience.

Dynamic Creative for Geo-Targeting:

Dynamic Content: Utilize dynamic creative to display location-specific information, such as store addresses or local offers, based on the user's location.

Personalized Experience: Ensure that users receive an ad experience that feels tailored to their location, increasing relevance and engagement.

By effectively employing geo-targeting strategies, you can tailor your Snapchat ads to specific audiences in local and global contexts, enhancing engagement, resonance, and overall campaign effectiveness.

* * *

CHAPTER 7: BUDGETING AND BIDDING DEMYSTIFIED

Decoding The Budget-Setting Process On Snapchat

Decoding the budget-setting process on Snapchat involves understanding the platform's options for allocating your advertising budget effectively. Here's a step-by-step guide to help you navigate this process:

1. Define Campaign Objectives:
Clearly define your campaign goals, whether it's brand awareness, conversions, app installs, or engagement. Your budget allocation will depend on your specific objectives.

2. Choose Ad Format:
Select the ad format that best aligns with your objectives and resonates with your target audience. Different formats may require varying budget allocations.

3. Set Campaign Budget:
Choose between two budget options: Daily Budget (the amount you're willing to spend per day) or Lifetime Budget (the total budget for the entire campaign duration). Ensure your budget is realistic based on your goals.

4. Set Ad Group Budget:
Within each campaign, you can have multiple ad groups targeting different audiences or objectives. Allocate a portion of your campaign budget to each

ad group.

5. Bid Strategy:

Choose a bid strategy that suits your objectives. Options include Automatic Bidding (Snapchat optimizes bids for your goals) or Target Cost Bidding (you set a specific cost per desired outcome).

6. Audience and Placement:

Refine your audience targeting and ad placement. This affects the potential reach and engagement, which in turn can influence your budget allocation.

7. Daily Cap:

Set a daily cap to ensure your spending remains within your desired limits. This option prevents exceeding your budget unexpectedly.

8. Ad Schedule:

Choose when your ads will be displayed. You can select specific days and times to maximize visibility during peak periods.

9. Optimization and Testing:

Start with a moderate budget to test performance. Monitor engagement, conversions, and other relevant metrics. Adjust budget allocations based on which ad groups or targeting options yield the best results.

10. Scaling:

If your initial results are promising, consider gradually increasing your budget to reach a wider audience. Continue to monitor performance as you scale up.

11. Flexibility:

Snapchat's budget settings allow for flexibility. You can adjust your budget, bid strategy, and targeting options during the campaign to optimize results.

12. Performance Monitoring:

Regularly review performance metrics such as impressions, click-through rates, conversions, and return on ad spend (ROAS). Use this data to refine your budget allocation strategy.

13. Experimentation:
Allocate a portion of your budget for experimentation. Test different ad creatives, targeting options, and bid strategies to find the most effective combination.

14. Cost Management:
Set realistic expectations for your budget and desired outcomes. Ensure that your cost per result aligns with your campaign goals and industry benchmarks.

By following these steps and monitoring the performance of your campaigns, you can effectively decode the budget-setting process on Snapchat and allocate your resources to achieve optimal results.

Bid Strategies Demystified: CPM, CPV, And Beyond

Demystifying bid strategies in the realm of Snapchat ads involves understanding key terms like CPM, CPV, and beyond. Here's a breakdown to help you navigate these concepts:

1. CPM (Cost per Mille):
CPM is a bid strategy where you pay for every 1,000 impressions your ad receives. This strategy is suitable for increasing brand visibility and awareness. It's ideal when your goal is to reach a wide audience and generate impressions.

2. CPV (Cost per View):
CPV is a bid strategy used for video ads, where you pay each time your video is viewed. On Snapchat, a view is counted when a video is watched for at least 2 seconds. CPV is effective when your objective is to engage users through video content.

3. CPC (Cost per Click):

CPC is a bid strategy where you pay when someone clicks on your ad. This is beneficial when your goal is to drive traffic to your website or landing page. It's a performance-based strategy that focuses on user interaction.

4. Target Cost Bidding:
This bid strategy allows you to set a specific cost per desired outcome, such as an app install or a conversion. Snapchat will adjust your bid to help you achieve that cost while optimizing delivery.

5. Maximum Bid Bidding:
With this strategy, you set the maximum amount you're willing to pay for an action, such as a click or impression. Snapchat will work to get you the best results within your set budget.

6. Minimum Bid:
Minimum bid is the lowest amount you're willing to pay for an action. Snapchat's auction system ensures that your ad competes fairly with others targeting the same audience.

7. Bid Amount and Budget:
Your bid amount and budget go hand in hand. A higher bid can lead to more visibility, but it might increase your cost. Your budget dictates how much you're willing to spend overall.

8. Real-Time Auctions:
Snapchat ad auctions occur in real-time when users match the targeting criteria of your ad. Advertisers with higher bids and quality content have a better chance of winning the auction.

9. Ad Relevance:
Alongside bid strategies, ad relevance is crucial. Relevant, engaging ads often perform better, leading to higher ad placements and lower costs.

10. Continuous Monitoring and Adjustment:
Regularly monitor your campaign's performance metrics, such as click-through rates, conversions, and cost per result. Adjust your bid strategies based on data insights to optimize outcomes.

11. A/B Testing:
Experiment with different bid strategies to find the one that aligns with your campaign goals. A/B testing can help you determine which strategy drives the best results.

12. Balance Objectives:
Choose a bid strategy that aligns with your campaign objectives. Consider your goals—whether it's brand awareness, engagement, conversions, or click-throughs—when making bid strategy decisions.

By understanding these bid strategies and their applications, you can make informed decisions when setting your bids for Snapchat ads and ensure that your campaigns are aligned with your desired outcomes.

Proven Techniques For Efficient Budget Allocation

Efficient budget allocation for Snapchat ads involves employing proven techniques that maximize the impact of your spending. Here are strategies to help you allocate your budget effectively:

1. Set Clear Objectives:
Define your campaign goals and prioritize them. Allocate a larger portion of your budget to objectives that directly contribute to your business's success, whether it's conversions, brand awareness, or engagement.

2. Test with Small Budgets:
Start with smaller budgets to test different ad formats, creatives, and targeting options. Gather performance data to identify which strategies are delivering the best results.

3. Focus on High-Performing Segments:
Once you identify successful strategies, allocate more budget to the high-performing ad sets or campaigns. Concentrate your resources where you're

seeing the most engagement and conversions.

4. Dayparting:

Analyze when your target audience is most active on Snapchat. Allocate a larger budget during those peak times to ensure your ads are seen when users are most likely to engage.

5. Geographic Targeting:

Allocate budget based on the geographic areas that are most relevant to your campaign. If you're running local promotions, focus on those areas. For global campaigns, distribute budget across regions strategically.

6. Bid Strategies:

Choose bid strategies that align with your objectives. For example, if your goal is engagement, CPV bidding might be more suitable. If conversions are the focus, consider target cost bidding.

7. Audience Segmentation:

Segment your audience based on demographics, interests, and behaviors. Allocate budget according to the size and potential of each segment. Prioritize high-converting groups.

8. Performance Monitoring:

Regularly review your campaign's performance metrics. Adjust your budget allocation based on which ad sets or audiences are generating the most engagement and conversions.

9. Split Testing:

Conduct split tests with different creatives, ad formats, and targeting options. Allocate budget evenly to these tests to identify the most effective combinations.

10. Scaling Gradually:

If a campaign is delivering strong results, consider gradually increasing the budget rather than making abrupt changes. Monitor how scaling affects performance.

11. Optimize Landing Pages:

Ensure that the landing pages your ads direct users to are optimized for conversions. A well-designed landing page can improve the efficiency of your ad spend.

12. Monitor Ad Fatigue:

Keep an eye on how often your target audience sees the same ad. Rotate and refresh your creatives to prevent ad fatigue, which can lead to decreased engagement.

13. Consider the Sales Funnel:

Allocate budget according to where your audience is in the sales funnel. More budget can be allocated to retargeting campaigns for users who are closer to conversion.

14. Regular Adjustments:

Be prepared to adjust your budget allocation throughout the campaign based on real-time performance data. Flexibility is key to optimizing outcomes.

By applying these proven techniques, you can strategically allocate your budget for Snapchat ads, ensuring that your spending aligns with your campaign objectives and yields optimal results.

* * *

CHAPTER 8: METRICS THAT MATTER: EVALUATING CAMPAIGN PERFORMANCE

Identifying Key Performance Indicators (KPIs) Tailored To Snapchat

Identifying key performance indicators (KPIs) tailored to Snapchat involves aligning your campaign goals with the metrics that best measure your success on the platform. Here's a step-by-step approach to help you pinpoint the right KPIs:

1. Define Your Campaign Objectives:
Begin by clearly outlining your campaign goals. Whether it's brand awareness, conversions, app installs, or engagement, your objectives will guide your choice of KPIs.

2. Match KPIs to Objectives:
Select KPIs that directly correspond to your campaign objectives. For instance, if you're aiming for brand awareness, KPIs like impressions and reach are relevant. If it's conversions, focus on metrics like click-through rates and conversion rates.

3. Consider Snapchat's Metrics:
Utilize Snapchat's native metrics that are specifically designed for the platform. These include Story Opens, Snap Completions, Swipe-Ups, and

more.

4. Engagement Metrics:
For engagement-focused campaigns, consider metrics like Story Completion Rates, which measure how many users watched your entire Story. Additionally, track the number of interactions with your filters, lenses, or other interactive elements.

5. Conversion Metrics:
For campaigns aiming for conversions, track metrics such as Click-Through Rates (CTR), Conversion Rates, and Return on Ad Spend (ROAS). These metrics provide insights into the effectiveness of your ads in driving users to take desired actions.

6. App Install Metrics:
If your goal is app installs, monitor metrics like Cost per Install (CPI) and Install Rate. These metrics help you understand the efficiency of your ad spend in driving app downloads.

7. Audience Engagement:
Evaluate metrics related to audience engagement, such as Likes, Shares, and Comments. These metrics reflect how users are interacting with your content.

8. Time-Sensitive Metrics:
For time-sensitive campaigns or events, track metrics like Story Views, which indicate the number of users who watched your story within a specific time frame.

9. Custom Metrics:
Consider creating custom metrics based on your unique campaign goals. For instance, if you're promoting a local event, you might measure the number of users who accessed your event details through a Web View Ad.

10. Performance Benchmarks:
Research industry benchmarks and Snapchat-specific averages to gauge the performance of your KPIs. This helps you set realistic expectations and

identify areas for improvement.

11. Align with Business Goals:
Ensure that the KPIs you choose align with your overall business objectives. The insights you gain from Snapchat campaigns should contribute to your broader business strategy.

12. Analyze Trends:
Regularly analyze the trends in your chosen KPIs. Identify patterns, spikes, or dips that can inform adjustments to your strategy.

13. Continuous Optimization:
Use your KPI data to optimize your campaigns. Experiment with different ad formats, targeting options, and creative variations to improve your KPI performance.

By aligning your KPIs with your campaign goals and utilizing Snapchat's platform-specific metrics, you can effectively measure the success of your campaigns and make informed decisions to enhance your performance on the platform.

Navigating Snapchat Ads Manager Analytics Toolkit

Navigating Snapchat Ads Manager Analytics Toolkit involves accessing valuable insights to assess your campaign performance and make informed decisions. Here's a step-by-step guide:

1. Access Ads Manager:
Log in to your Snapchat Ads Manager account. If you're new to Snapchat advertising, you'll need to create an account.

2. Campaign Overview:
Upon login, you'll see a dashboard displaying an overview of your active campaigns. You can view key metrics such as spend, impressions, and click-through rates.

3. Campaign Breakdown:

Click on a specific campaign to access more detailed insights. You'll see ad sets and ads within that campaign, along with metrics specific to each.

4. Analytics Toolkit:

Look for the Analytics Toolkit, which provides deeper insights into your campaign performance. This toolkit houses various metrics and data visualization tools.

5. Performance Metrics:

Explore metrics such as Impressions, Reach, Click-Through Rate (CTR), Conversion Rate, Cost per Result, and more. These metrics help you understand user engagement and campaign efficiency.

6. Customizable Date Range:

Adjust the date range to analyze campaign performance over a specific period. You can compare data across different timeframes to identify trends.

7. Graphs and Charts:

The Analytics Toolkit offers visual representations of your data through graphs and charts. These visuals make it easier to spot patterns and changes in performance.

8. Filters and Grouping:

Utilize filters and grouping options to segment your data. You can group data by campaign objective, ad set, placement, or other relevant categories.

9. Export Reports:

If you need to share insights or analyze data externally, consider exporting reports. Snapchat Ads Manager allows you to download reports in various formats.

10. Breakdown by Platform:

Analyze how your ads are performing on different platforms, such as Snapchat's Discover, Stories, and more. This breakdown helps you understand where your audience engages most.

11. Audience Insights:
Access audience insights to understand demographics, interests, and behaviors of users interacting with your ads. This information aids in refining your targeting strategy.

12. Optimization Suggestions:
Snapchat Ads Manager might offer optimization suggestions based on your campaign performance. Consider these suggestions to improve your ad's effectiveness.

13. Iterative Optimization:
Regularly review your campaign's performance using the Analytics Toolkit. Make iterative adjustments to your strategy based on data insights.

14. Learning Resources:
If you're new to Snapchat Ads Manager, utilize learning resources provided by Snapchat. These resources offer guidance on interpreting metrics and improving performance.

15. Experiment and Iterate:
Experiment with different ad formats, targeting options, and bid strategies. Use the Analytics Toolkit to assess the impact of these changes.

By navigating Snapchat Ads Manager Analytics Toolkit effectively, you can gain a comprehensive understanding of your campaign's performance, identify areas for improvement, and make data-driven decisions to optimize your Snapchat ad strategy.

Extracting Actionable Insights To Refine Your Strategies

Extracting actionable insights from your Snapchat campaigns involves analyzing data to inform strategic refinements. Here's how to do it effectively:

1. Define Clear Objectives:
Start by revisiting your campaign goals. Identify which metrics align with your objectives, whether it's engagement, conversions, or brand awareness.

2. Identify Key Metrics:
Focus on key performance indicators (KPIs) that directly relate to your goals. These could include metrics like CTR, conversion rate, or impressions.

3. Comparative Analysis:
Compare data across different time periods, ad sets, or demographics. Look for trends, spikes, or dips in performance.

4. Audience Insights:
Understand your audience demographics, interests, and behaviors. This helps refine targeting and tailor content to resonate with your users.

5. A/B Testing:
Analyze the results of A/B tests. Compare different ad variations to identify what resonates best with your audience.

6. Conversion Funnel:
Trace the user journey from ad view to conversion. Identify drop-off points and optimize those stages for a smoother conversion process.

7. Engagement Patterns:
Study user engagement patterns. Which types of content or ad formats receive the most interaction? Use this insight to guide content creation.

8. Ad Placement Analysis:
Evaluate the performance of ads in different placements (Discover, Stories, etc.). Allocate budget to placements that yield the best results.

9. Geo-Performance:
Examine how ads perform in different geographic locations. Adjust content or targeting based on regional engagement.

10. Audience Retention:
Analyze how long users engage with your content. Optimize your ad's length and structure to retain audience attention.

11. Return on Investment (ROI):
Calculate ROI by comparing ad spend with revenue generated. This metric informs the profitability of your campaigns.

12. Attribution Analysis:
Understand which touchpoints contribute to conversions. Assess the effectiveness of various channels in the user's journey.

13. Seasonal Trends:
Identify seasonal trends that affect engagement. Adjust your content and campaigns to align with these patterns.

14. Iterative Optimization:
Use insights to make iterative adjustments to your campaigns. Tweak targeting, creatives, or bidding strategies based on data trends.

15. Continuous Learning:
Stay updated with Snapchat's updates, features, and case studies. Apply relevant findings to enhance your strategies.

16. Benchmarking:
Compare your campaign performance with industry benchmarks. This provides context and helps you set realistic goals.

17. Feedback Loop:
Communicate with your team to gather insights from different perspectives. Collaborative analysis can uncover valuable insights.

18. Experimentation:
Continue to experiment with new ideas and strategies. Use data from previous campaigns to refine your approach.

By consistently extracting actionable insights from your Snapchat campaigns, you can fine-tune your strategies, optimize performance, and ensure that your efforts align with your goals and deliver optimal results.

* * *

CHAPTER 9: EVOLUTION THROUGH OPTIMIZATION: A/B TESTING MASTERY

Unveiling The Power Of Split Testing Ad Variants

Unveiling the power of split-testing ad variants in Snapchat ads involves a systematic approach to compare different ad elements and optimize your campaigns. Here's how to effectively conduct split tests:

1. Clear Goal Definition:
Start by defining a clear goal for your split test. Whether it's improving CTR, conversions, or engagement, having a specific objective guides your testing strategy.

2. Identify Test Variables:
Choose the elements you want to test. This could include ad copy, visuals, headlines, CTAs, ad formats, and even audience targeting.

3. Create Variants:
Develop multiple ad variants, each featuring a single change. For example, if testing ad copy, keep visuals consistent while altering the text.

4. Audience Segmentation:
Divide your audience into groups that are statistically significant for testing. Ensure each group represents a similar demographic and behavior profile.

5. Implement Control Group:

Include a control group that receives the current version of your ad. This helps establish a baseline for comparison.

6. Time and Rotation:

Distribute ad variants evenly over a specific period to account for any temporal variations. Rotate ad display to minimize biases.

7. Track Key Metrics:

Monitor key performance metrics for each ad variant, such as CTR, conversion rate, and engagement. Compare these metrics to determine the most effective variant.

8. Statistical Significance:

Ensure that your sample size is statistically significant to draw valid conclusions. Tools and calculators are available to help determine significance.

9. Analyze Results:

Compare the performance of ad variants against the control group. Identify patterns, trends, and significant differences in metrics.

10. Iterative Changes:

Based on the results, implement changes to your campaigns. Scale up successful variants and discard underperforming ones.

11. Learn and Apply:

Use insights gained from split testing to refine your overall ad strategy. Apply lessons learned to future campaigns.

12. Continuous Testing:

Split testing is an ongoing process. Continuously test new hypotheses and adapt your strategy based on real-time data.

13. Data-Driven Decisions:

Let data guide your decisions. Avoid making changes solely based on assumptions; rely on evidence from split testing.

14. Creative Elements:
Test a variety of creative elements, such as imagery, colors, fonts, and ad format variations. Determine which combination resonates best with your audience.

15. Ad Copy:
Experiment with different ad copy tones, lengths, and messaging approaches. Discover which wording prompts higher engagement.

16. Seasonal Relevance:
Consider testing ad variants that are seasonally relevant. Tailoring your content to specific periods can enhance audience resonance.

17. Feedback Incorporation:
Gather feedback from your team and users. This can provide insights for potential changes to test in future campaigns.

By embracing split testing as a powerful tool, you can uncover valuable insights, refine your Snapchat ad strategies, and consistently optimize your campaigns for better performance and results.

Strategically Experimenting With Visuals, Headlines, And CTAs

Strategically experimenting with visuals, headlines, and CTAs in Snapchat ads involves a systematic approach to testing and optimizing these crucial elements. Here's a step-by-step guide to help you conduct effective experiments:

1. Clear Objectives:
Begin by defining clear objectives for your experiments. Whether it's increasing engagement, conversions, or brand awareness, having a specific

goal guides your testing.

2. Visual Variations:
Create multiple ad variations with different visuals. Test various imagery, colors, and layouts to identify what resonates best with your audience.

3. Headline Testing:
Craft different headlines for your ad variants. Experiment with tones, lengths, and messaging to determine which headlines attract the most attention.

4. CTA Alternatives:
Develop various Call-to-Action (CTA) options. Test different action-oriented phrases to find the one that drives the most clicks or conversions.

5. A/B Testing:
Divide your audience into groups and present them with different ad variants. Ensure that each group is statistically significant to draw valid conclusions.

6. Controlled Variables:
Keep other elements consistent while testing visuals, headlines, or CTAs. This ensures that any observed differences are attributed to the variables you're testing.

7. Implement a Schedule:
Rotate ad variants evenly over a specific timeframe to account for temporal variations. This helps eliminate biases in performance.

8. Tracking Metrics:
Monitor key performance metrics such as Click-Through Rates (CTR), conversion rates, and engagement. Compare these metrics to identify trends.

9. Statistical Significance:
Ensure that your sample size is statistically significant before drawing conclusions. Utilize statistical tools to determine significance.

10. Analyze Data:

Examine the performance of each ad element variation. Identify patterns and differences in metrics to understand which elements are driving better results.

11. Hypothesis Testing:

Formulate hypotheses based on the outcomes of your experiments. Develop insights into why certain visuals, headlines, or CTAs performed better.

12. Optimize and Refine:

Use insights gained from experimentation to optimize your ad campaigns. Scale up the successful elements and incorporate them into your strategy.

13. Continuous Iteration:

Recognize that experimentation is an ongoing process. Continuously test new combinations and elements to stay relevant and engaging.

14. Audience Feedback:

Seek feedback from your target audience. Conduct surveys or engage with users to gather insights on what resonates with them.

15. Seasonal Adaptations:

Adapt your visuals, headlines, and CTAs to align with seasonal trends, holidays, or events. Tailoring content can enhance relevance and engagement.

16. Data-Driven Decisions:

Base your decisions on data rather than assumptions. Let the results of your experiments guide your choices.

17. Collaborative Approach:

Involve your team in brainstorming and analyzing experiments. Different perspectives can provide valuable insights.

By strategically experimenting with visuals, headlines, and CTAs in your Snapchat ads, you can uncover insights that lead to more effective campaigns, higher engagement, and better overall performance.

Continuous Improvement Methodologies For Lasting Success

Using continuous improvement methodologies for lasting success in Snapchat ads involves adopting a systematic approach to refine and enhance your campaigns over time. Here's a step-by-step guide to implementing these methodologies:

1. Set Clear Goals:
Define specific goals for your Snapchat ad campaigns. These objectives guide your continuous improvement efforts and provide a clear direction.

2. Regular Analysis:
Consistently monitor campaign performance using Snapchat's analytics tools. Regularly review key metrics like CTR, conversion rates, and engagement.

3. Identify Areas for Improvement:
Analyze performance data to identify areas that require improvement. Look for patterns, trends, and deviations from your goals.

4. Experimentation:
Experiment with different ad elements, targeting options, and bidding strategies. Use A/B testing to systematically test changes and measure their impact.

5. Iterative Optimization:
Based on experimentation, make incremental changes to your campaigns. Continuously refine ad copy, visuals, and targeting to enhance performance.

6. Data-Driven Decisions:
Base your decisions on data rather than assumptions. Let the insights gained from analytics drive your optimization strategy.

7. Learn from Insights:

Extract actionable insights from your analytics. Use these insights to understand user behavior and preferences, guiding your future decisions.

8. Audience Feedback:

Engage with your audience to gather feedback on ad content and user experience. User input can provide valuable insights for improvement.

9. Collaborative Approach:

Involve your team in the continuous improvement process. Different perspectives contribute to comprehensive analysis and creative solutions.

10. Implement Best Practices:

Stay updated on best practices for Snapchat advertising. Apply industry insights and trends to optimize your campaigns.

11. Adaptive Campaigns:

Adapt your campaigns based on changing trends, seasonal shifts, or shifts in user behavior. Flexibility ensures your content remains relevant.

12. Quality Assurance:

Regularly review your ad creatives and ensure they align with your brand identity and messaging. High-quality content contributes to better results.

13. Performance Benchmarks:

Compare your campaign results against industry benchmarks. This provides context for your performance and helps you set realistic goals.

14. Document Insights:

Document the insights gained from your continuous improvement efforts. This knowledge base can guide future campaigns and strategies.

15. Incremental Changes:

Make small, incremental changes to your campaigns. This allows you to assess the impact of each change individually.

16. Regular Review:

Set aside time for regular campaign reviews and optimization. Consistency in analyzing and refining your campaigns leads to lasting success.

17. Stay Curious and Adaptable:

Stay curious about new strategies, features, and trends. Be adaptable in implementing changes based on emerging opportunities.

By incorporating continuous improvement methodologies into your Snapchat ad campaigns, you create a cycle of refinement that leads to lasting success. Regular analysis, experimentation, and optimization contribute to enhanced performance, increased engagement, and improved ROI over time.

* * *

CHAPTER 10: TRAILBLAZING AHEAD: ADVANCED TACTICS AND EMERGING TRENDS

Elevating Campaigns With Advanced Retargeting Strategies

Elevating your Snapchat ad campaigns with advanced retargeting strategies involves employing targeted approaches to re-engage users who have previously interacted with your brand. Here's a guide to help you implement advanced retargeting:

1. Audience Segmentation:
Segment your audience based on their interactions with your brand. Create lists for users who visited your website, engaged with previous ads, or abandoned a shopping cart.

2. Custom Audience Creation:
Utilize Snapchat's Custom Audience feature to upload lists of customer emails or phone numbers. This enables you to retarget users directly.

3. Lookalike Audiences:
Leverage Lookalike Audiences to reach users similar to your existing customers. Snapchat identifies common traits and behaviors to expand your

target reach.

4. Dynamic Product Ads:
Implement Dynamic Product Ads to automatically show users products they previously viewed on your website or app. This personalizes the ad experience.

5. Event Tracking:
Integrate Snapchat with your website or app using event tracking. This allows you to retarget users who performed specific actions, such as adding items to a wishlist.

6. Sequential Messaging:
Craft a sequence of ads that tells a story or guides users through the sales funnel. Start with brand awareness and gradually move towards conversion-focused ads.

7. Cart Abandonment Strategy:
Retarget users who abandoned their shopping carts. Show them targeted ads featuring the products they left behind, along with incentives to complete the purchase.

8. Frequency Capping:
Set frequency caps to prevent overexposure. This ensures retargeting ads remain relevant and engaging without becoming intrusive.

9. Seasonal Retargeting:
Tailor retargeting campaigns to specific seasons or events. Promote relevant offers based on user behavior during those times.

10. Time-Based Retargeting:
Adjust retargeting timing based on user behavior. For example, target users who recently visited your site with a reminder ad shortly after their visit.

11. Cross-Platform Retargeting:
Extend retargeting efforts across multiple platforms. Consistent messaging reinforces your brand and encourages user action.

12. Exclusion Lists:

Create exclusion lists to avoid retargeting users who have already converted or taken the desired action. This prevents irrelevant ads.

13. Performance Monitoring:

Regularly monitor the performance of your retargeting campaigns. Analyze metrics like click-through rates, conversions, and ROI to gauge success.

14. Iterative Optimization:

Based on performance data, optimize your retargeting strategies. Adjust ad creative, targeting parameters, and bid strategies to improve results.

15. A/B Testing:

Conduct A/B tests with different ad creatives and messaging. Discover which retargeting approaches yield the highest engagement and conversions.

16. Compliance and Transparency:

Adhere to privacy regulations and provide transparent opt-out options for users who wish to discontinue retargeting.

By implementing advanced retargeting strategies in your Snapchat ad campaigns, you can effectively re-engage users, nurture them through the sales funnel, and achieve better campaign performance and ROI.

Immersive Experiences With Augmented Reality (AR) Ads

Utilizing immersive experiences with augmented reality (AR) ads in Snapchat involves creating interactive and engaging campaigns that leverage AR technology. Here's a guide to help you effectively use AR ads:

1. Understand Your Audience:

Identify your target audience's preferences and behaviors to tailor AR experiences that resonate with them.

2. Choose the Right Ad Format:
Select the appropriate AR ad format for your campaign, such as Sponsored Lenses or Filters. Each format offers different ways to engage users.

3. Develop Creative Concepts:
Brainstorm creative ideas that align with your brand and campaign goals. AR ads should provide value, entertainment, or utility to users.

4. Leverage Snapchat's AR Tools:
Explore Snapchat's AR tools and features, like Lens Studio, to design and develop interactive AR experiences. These tools make it accessible for advertisers to create engaging content.

5. Encourage User Interaction:
Design AR ads that encourage users to actively engage with the experience. Incorporate calls to action that prompt them to interact and share.

6. Showcase Products Virtually:
If applicable, integrate product visualization into AR experiences. Users can try on makeup virtually, visualize furniture in their space, or see how a product fits their lifestyle.

7. Align with Brand Identity:
Ensure your AR experience aligns with your brand's tone, aesthetics, and messaging. Consistency enhances brand recognition.

8. User-Friendly Interface:
Keep the AR interaction intuitive and user-friendly. Users should be able to understand and engage with the experience easily.

9. Solve User Problems:
Create AR experiences that solve a problem or fulfill a need for users. This could be trying out makeup shades, virtually test-driving a car, or visualizing home improvements.

10. Storytelling through AR:
Craft narratives that unfold through AR interactions. Users can be guided through a storyline that immerses them in your brand's message.

11. Gamification Elements:
Incorporate gamified elements like challenges, quizzes, or mini-games into your AR experiences. This boosts engagement and adds an element of fun.

12. Social Sharing Integration:
Enable users to easily share their AR experiences on social media. User-generated content can extend the reach of your campaign.

13. Real-World Integration:
Design AR ads that seamlessly integrate with the user's environment. This enhances the sense of immersion and realism.

14. Measure Performance:
Monitor key metrics such as engagement rate, time spent interacting with the AR ad, and social shares. Analyze the impact of AR on campaign success.

15. Iterative Improvement:
Based on performance data, refine your AR experiences. Optimize elements that drive the most engagement and positive user feedback.

16. Ad Transparency and Relevance:
Ensure that your AR ads are relevant to the user experience and transparent about the purpose of the interaction.

By effectively utilizing immersive experiences with AR ads on Snapchat, you can captivate your audience, drive engagement, and create memorable interactions that strengthen your brand's connection with users.

Gazing Into The Future: Snapchat's Evolving Landscape And Trends

To adapt to Snapchat's evolving landscape and trends in the future, it's crucial to stay agile and proactive. Here's how you can prepare for changes and remain relevant:

1. Stay Informed:
Continuously monitor Snapchat's updates, features, and announcements. Being aware of platform changes will help you anticipate shifts in the landscape.

2. Embrace Innovation:
Stay open to adopting new ad formats, technologies, and creative approaches that Snapchat introduces. Experiment with innovative features to engage users.

3. Flexibility in Strategy:
Be prepared to adjust your ad strategy based on emerging trends and user behaviors. Flexibility allows you to adapt quickly to changing preferences.

4. Analyze Data:
Regularly analyze performance data and user insights. Data-driven decisions are key to adapting to what's working and what's not.

5. Experimentation Mindset:
Embrace a culture of experimentation. Test new ideas, creatives, and targeting options to discover what resonates with your audience.

6. Audience-Centric Approach:
Keep your audience's preferences, behaviors, and demographics at the forefront of your strategy. Adapt to their changing needs and expectations.

7. Future-Proof Creatives:
Create evergreen and adaptable ad creatives that can be tweaked for different trends. This saves time and ensures relevance.

8. Early Adoption:
Where relevant, consider early adoption of new Snapchat features. This positions you as an innovative brand and allows you to learn and optimize

early on.

9. User-Generated Content:
Leverage user-generated content and trends. This not only aligns with current movements but also fosters a sense of community engagement.

10. Build Relationships:
Build strong relationships with your Snapchat account manager or representatives. They can provide insights and guidance on upcoming trends.

11. Competitive Analysis:
Monitor your competitors' Snapchat campaigns. This can offer insights into strategies that are gaining traction and help you differentiate.

12. Storytelling Evolution:
Adapt your storytelling techniques to new trends. As user preferences change, your narratives should remain fresh and relevant.

13. Diversified Content:
Diversify your content strategy to encompass different ad formats, from AR to interactive experiences, keeping up with user expectations.

14. Consistent Monitoring:
Regularly review your campaigns and strategies. Trends can change rapidly, and consistent monitoring helps you avoid falling behind.

15. Network and Community Engagement:
Engage with the Snapchat community, participate in relevant discussions, and network with fellow advertisers. This can uncover valuable insights.

16. Strategic Partnerships:
Explore collaborations with influencers or other brands. Strategic partnerships can help amplify your presence within evolving trends.

Adapting to Snapchat's evolving landscape and trends requires a proactive, forward-thinking mindset. By staying informed, embracing innovation, and remaining flexible in your approach, you can ensure that your Snapchat ad campaigns continue to resonate with users and deliver meaningful results in the ever-changing digital landscape.

CONCLUSION

As we draw the curtains on our journey through the realm of Snapchat advertising, you now possess a comprehensive toolkit to wield this dynamic platform with finesse and confidence. "Snapchat Ads Blueprint: Your Strategy For Unmatched Marketing Impact," has been your steadfast companion, illuminating the path from novice to adept in the art of crafting compelling campaigns.

Through these chapters, we've dismantled the intricacies of Snapchat's advertising ecosystem, demystifying its ad formats, targeting techniques, and analytics intricacies. Your understanding of this platform's potential is now honed, and your ability to strategize, execute, and optimize campaigns has been elevated.

However, our voyage does not conclude here. In the rapidly evolving landscape of digital marketing, adaptation is key. Snapchat's potential continues to grow, and its creative canvas is ever-expanding. The future holds opportunities yet unexplored, and emerging trends beckon the curious and bold. As a master of Snapchat advertising, you're well-positioned to seize these opportunities, armed with the knowledge to innovate and lead the way.

Remember, successful marketing on Snapchat isn't just about mastering tools and metrics; it's about understanding the hearts and minds of your audience. It's about capturing their attention, weaving narratives that resonate, and fostering genuine connections in a world flooded with content. Your journey isn't just about mastering Snapchat ads; it's about connecting with people, leaving an impact, and driving meaningful results for your brand.

So, as you navigate your way forward, continue to experiment, iterate, and evolve your strategies. Embrace change, for it is the harbinger of growth. Stay attuned to shifts in user behavior, emerging technologies, and the pulse of your audience. Your success will always be a reflection of your ability to adapt and innovate.

With newfound knowledge and a vision fueled by creativity, data, and insight, you're poised to reshape the narrative of your brand in the minds of Snapchat's vast audience. As the digital landscape transforms, you stand not only as a master of Snapchat advertising but also as a trailblazer, a storyteller, and a driving force of change.

Go forth with confidence, ambition, and the tools you've gained within these pages. The world of Snapchat awaits your ingenuity, your creativity, and your unwavering dedication to excellence in marketing. May your campaigns be vibrant, your engagement be lasting, and your impact be profound.

Thank you for embarking on this journey with "Snapchat Ads Blueprint: Your Strategy For Unmatched Marketing Impact." Your pursuit of mastery is an inspiration, and your potential is boundless. Here's to your continued success in the ever-evolving world of Snapchat advertising.

And as an added bonus, scan the QR code below for a lifetime coupon of 10% for any t-shirt purchase. Just apply the code BOOK at checkout.